Survival in Cyberspace

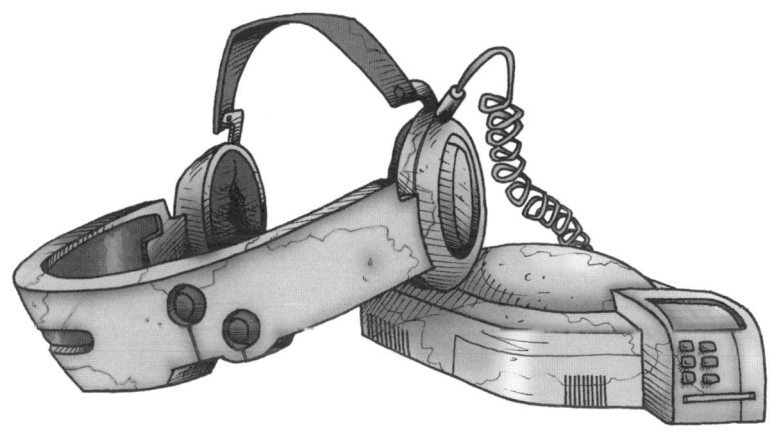

Written by Angie Belcher
Illustrated by Alan Cochrane

	...5
Chapter 1	...20
Chapter 2	...28
Chapter 3	...37
Chapter 4	...47
Chapter 5	...53
Chapter 6	...64
Chapter 7	...69
Chapter 8	...75
Chapter 9	...83
Chapter 10	...92
Glossary	

CHAPTER 1

From Jen's hidden perch on the branch of a densely needled pine tree, she could see over the tall security wall that wrapped around Future-Tech Laboratory.

To Jen's left was the reinforced security control station, watched over twenty-four hours a day by a security guard.

Jen had noticed a few changes in laboratory routine during the past week. Strangely, Dr. Linden had replaced the day guard in the security station. Dr. Linden had long been known in the community for her brilliance in computer technology. Why she had ever been moved to security guard operations was beyond Jen's comprehension.

Dr. Linden stayed inside the station, her face bathed in the glow of video screens, her fingers restlessly playing over the control panel. There had been a rumor about information leaks in Dr. Linden's division. Had they demoted her to teach her a lesson?

Jen never tired of hanging around the laboratory. She loved to imagine the technology within its walls and dreamed of entering a world of bytes and chips. She longed to create a wonderful new software that would change the world. The world of technology was her escape from reality. As far as she was concerned, anywhere was better than being at home or school.

The sound of an approaching car startled Jen. She scooted back further into the dense foliage, then watched as the car glided to a halt. She tried to make out the shapes of the people hidden behind the tinted glass but could see nothing. Dr. Linden leaned out the window of the security station. The driver's window slid down and a hand reached out and placed itself on the Perspex panel that protruded from the side of the station.

The panel flashed as it rapidly scanned the driver's handprint. "Identity confirmed. Clearance approved. Proceed," intoned a computerized voice. The tall steel gates slid apart and Dr. Linden waved the car through.

Jen watched the car proceed through the laboratory complex. That's odd, she thought. That's the third time I've seen that vehicle come or go this week. I wonder what's going on? She craned her neck to see more.

The snapping of twigs directly beneath the tree made Jen's heart leap into her throat. She looked down through a gap in the branches at Dr. Linden's stern face peering up at her.

"That's enough prying," Dr. Linden said. "Get down from there."

Jen looked down at the security guard. "I wasn't doing anything," she stammered, embarrassed at being discovered.

"Look, you've got to quit hanging around here. It looks suspicious. You're going to get us both in a heap of trouble."

"But no one can see me, Dr. Linden."

"*I* saw you. And someone else might, too. Now I want you to get down and get back to school. The lunch break is almost over. You don't want to be absent from any classes."

"But, Dr. Linden, school really stinks. That computer work they make us do is kids' stuff. If I have to write another basic visual program or create another database I'll scream. Couldn't you just get me into the labs for a quick look? Please! Just once! I promise I won't tell anyone, and I'll keep away afterward. I just want to see inside."

"Jen, the only way you'll ever get inside those walls is to go to school and keep working on your computer skills. And if I were you, I'd get back before anyone realizes you're gone." Dr. Linden seemed to be trying hard to sound angry.

Jen climbed down. "OK, OK, I'm off," she called over her shoulder as she hurried down the road toward school. She couldn't afford to be late again. The last thing she wanted was for someone to contact Mom at work. Things were tough enough for her since Dad had left.

The afternoon loomed ahead of her like a dark cloud. Intermediate Databasing and Basic Visual.

With classes like that to look forward to, Jen thought, why even get up in the morning?

When Jen arrived home that afternoon, she went straight to her room. A large flat computer screen hung on the wall over her desk, displaying constantly changing landscapes. "Yeah, I wish I were there," she murmured as an image of sand dunes and blazing sunlight flicked onto the screen.

"Come on, Fireball," she said to the tiny red kitten winding itself over her feet and through her legs. "Let's go surf the Net. That's more interesting than the kids' stuff they do at school."

She picked up the kitten and sat at the desk, triggering the computer's voice activator. "Identify yourself," droned the mechanical voice.

"Come on, you know me by now. 'Surfin' Jen, your Internet friend,'" said Jen.

"Voice identity confirmed," replied the computer humorlessly. "Print identification please."

Jen placed her index finger on a pad set at the base of the screen.

"Identification confirmed. Hello, Jen. How are you? Where are we going today? Virtual Videos on Venezuela? Disc Downloads from Denali? Audio Amplifications of Australian Aborigines?" The list went on and on as more choices scrolled across the screen.

These new computers are the greatest, thought Jen. Who says computers are antisocial? I get more meaningful conversation from this collection of chips than I get from anyone at school.

Jen had always felt different from other kids, what with her frizzy red hair, freckles, glasses, braces, and brains – lots of brains, *too* many brains. "Jughead Jen, Techno-Twit," the other kids teased. After too many years of this teasing, Jen had stopped trying to make friends. Especially after her father left. If any of the other kids mentioned *that*, it usually meant a fight and a trip to the principal's office. There, Jen would receive another lecture about "you're a very intelligent young lady. I just don't understand why you…"

Yuck, thought Jen, shaking her head. Who needs it? She turned her attention to her kitten.

"Let's get to it, Fireball." The kitten looked up from her perch on Jen's knees and purred contentedly.

"Take me traveling today," Jen told the computer. "I want to be as far away from here as possible." The computer whizzed and whirred as it connected with millions of network signals.

Almost instantly a list of travel sites appeared on the screen. "You have 123,359,209 hits," the computer's robotic voice informed her. "List will not be sorted. More information necessary."

"Hmmm," Jen muttered. "Let's try travel and adventure," she said. An even longer list of possibilities scrolled over the screen.

"Too many for me, Fireball. Here, you choose," said Jen. She closed her eyes, lifted the kitten, and let it bat at the screen.

KIDSAFE Travel Seekers
A site for children interested in
really going places

A series of image icons from around the world started flashing on the screen. Jen touched the

"Africa" icon. "African Adventure World" blazed in bright letters at the top of the screen. A few seconds later, a herd of elephants thundered its way toward her. The sound of the herd sent vibrations pounding through the computer's speakers. Fireball meowed loudly, leaped off Jen's lap, and disappeared under the bed.

"Cool!" Jen exclaimed.

At the bottom of the screen a number of headings flashed invitingly.

More Information	**Back to Home**
More Pages Like This	**Chat Room**

"Hey, Fireball," Jen said. The kitten had timidly reappeared and was now rubbing itself against Jen's leg. "Let's enter the chat room and see if anyone's there." The kitten jumped up onto her lap, meowing loudly.

"Now, now," Jen continued, "it's not that you're bad company. I'd just like to talk to someone."

She touched the "Chat Room" icon. "Do you want to maintain identity?" the computer asked as a bright beam of light shone from an area on the screen directly into Jen's left eye. "Retinal identity confirmed," the computer continued. "Access approved."

Jen knew it was not a good idea to give away too much information on the computer, even in a KIDSAFE zone. To gain access to a KIDSAFE zone, you had to register through IDENTIKIT with proof of age between seven and twelve. Any younger, you had to register with CHILDSAFE, any older (up to nineteen), TEENSAFE. Access was available only after a retinal scan.

Still, Jen realized, there were some kids just dying to gather personal information and use it for mischief. One of the kids at school had had his entire class record wiped out. It had taken forever to sort it out.

Jen didn't like to show her image or give away her address or personal information. After all, she thought, anything can happen.

"Connect me incognito," Jen told the computer. "No trace. No tracking."

A panel appeared on the screen.

Choose IDENTIKIT Alias and Username

Jen thought this was the best part of being in a chat room. She could call herself whatever she wanted and build a new persona using the features provided. "Username: Sidney Sidewinder," she said. "IDENTIKIT Features: female, straight dark hair, blue eyes."

An image appeared in a window on the screen. Jen tweaked it a few times. Not bad, she thought. I wish my hair was that straight.

She touched the "Join" icon. A series of windows appeared on the screen. Four of them held images of the chat room users. The remainder were blank.

"You have entered the KIDSAFE Travel Seekers Chat Room. Current users: four," the computer intoned. Each of the images had the username displayed beneath it. Jen almost didn't recognize her own IDENTIKIT picture. She watched as the occupants continued their conversation.

> **Amanda Moveover:** *Has anyone traveled recently?*
>
> **Nicolette Noisemaker:** *Oh yes, I've just returned from Patagonia. I was helping my mom film some Imax footage of killer whales to be used in a 3-D Virtual Reality Imax Theater.*
>
> **Ophelia Shakespeare:** *Wow! I bet that was exciting. I saw some orca images on a wildlife web site a few days ago.*

Jen had listened for just a few moments when one of the users spoke to her: *Welcome to the Travel Seekers Chat Room, Sidney.*

Sidney? Who is Sidney? wondered Jen before she suddenly remembered that was her username.

"Er, hi," she replied, the computer translating her voice onto the screen.

> **Amanda Moveover:** *Have you traveled anywhere interesting lately, Sidney?*

Jen looked at the image in the window. Amanda had dark hair and wore diamond studs in both ears. Hmmm, looks interesting enough, thought Jen. But what can you tell from an IDENTIKIT picture?

Jen hesitated. She'd appear boring if she said she'd never been anywhere. And after all, no one knew her or could see her. She could say whatever she wanted. No one would know the difference if she said she had accompanied an archaeologist returning from the Great Pyramid of Cheops or been on a family backpacking trip in Bengal.

Sidney Sidewinder: *Yes, in fact I have. I'm still jet-lagged! I've just returned from helping my dad, who was heading a group of scientists on board the research ship* Vincent Gaddis *in the Bermuda Triangle region of the Sargasso Sea. They were testing for magnetic fields that might explain the disappearance of planes and ships during the twentieth century. The data they recorded on the latest computer systems developed by*

> *Future-Tech Laboratory backs up their theories on the disappearances.*
>
> **Amanda Moveover:** *Hey, that sounds amazing. I heard that Future-Tech is developing all sorts of radical new software. I'd give anything to hack into one of their computer systems and see what's going on. I read somewhere that they are developing software for molecular transfer. You know* – real virtual reality, where they beam you live from one place to another.
>
> **Sidney Sidewinder:** *Wouldn't that be something? That would give a whole new meaning to adventure travel.*

Jen soon lost all concept of time and place as she joined the other chat room occupants in sharing ideas and travel adventures. Only the sudden slamming of the front door and the sound of her mother's footsteps brought her back to reality. Jen quickly turned to the screen and began to speak.

Sidney Sidewinder: *Sorry, Seekers, I'll have to disconnect... Uhm, my pet anaconda – the one I brought back from a recent trip to the Amazon – needs to be fed. I'll be back same time, same place tomorrow, if any of you can make it.*

As Jen strolled to school the next morning, she lingered longer than usual outside the wall surrounding Future-Tech.

"Get along now," Dr. Linden called, sounding less friendly than usual.

Jen could see the same official looking car approaching in the distance. When Dr. Linden looked toward it, Jen ducked out of sight, ran through the stand of trees, and shimmied back up to her spy perch.

The vehicle stopped for much longer than seemed necessary outside the gates. Judging by what Jen could see of Dr. Linden's face, something was going on. Jen began to feel uneasy as the car idled and Dr. Linden spoke to the driver. Finally, the car door opened just a fraction and Jen saw a black briefcase being shoved out. Dr. Linden snatched the briefcase and placed it out of sight in the security station.

Jen wondered what it was all about. It was odd that Dr. Linden hadn't asked for the driver's ID or used the Perspex handprint scanner to confirm the security clearance. Jen paused in her thoughts. Was Dr. Linden a spy?

She heard the school bell in the distance and quietly slipped down the tree and ran off to school. She could hardly wait to tell everyone in the tech lab about the Travel Seekers site. As soon as she arrived at school, she burst into the lab.

In the lab, the students were chattering and muttering and singing and yelling at the computer screens, playing different games and downloading techno-funk music into portable Discwalkers.

Many students wore virtual reality headsets with visor screens and earphones. Jen watched as they rocked and jerked violently from side to side. She wondered which virtual reality discs they were using. After watching the other kids for a while, she changed her mind about telling anyone about the chat room. Everyone seemed far more concerned with using computers as toys than as links to their future.

There were no spare machines, so Jen browsed aimlessly through the rows of travel discs and dreamed of visiting exotic places far away from home and school. Her first class was Database Formats, her second, Organizing with Basic Visual. The day dragged on and on. Jen couldn't wait to get home.

When she passed the Future-Tech complex that afternoon, Jen noticed a large van moving quickly away from the security station. As the van passed, she could see a shadowy figure on the passenger side, leafing through a mass of papers.

"Lots of action today?" Jen called out to Dr. Linden, who was standing at the door of the security station with a briefcase in her hand. "What's in the briefcase?"

Dr. Linden looked down as if just remembering what she held in her hand. She looked flustered. "That's really none of your business, Jen. You just keep yourself offline. I'll tell you when I want you to log on."

Jen laughed. She liked the way Dr. Linden sometimes dropped bits of techno-talk into their conversations.

"Someone in my chat group on the Travel Seekers site was telling me about Future-Tech. She mentioned some software that could complete molecular transfer," Jen babbled excitedly. "Wouldn't that be something?"

Dr. Linden looked at her strangely. "You're spending far too much time hanging around here, Jen. You never know when a stray virus might leak out and get into your system!"

Jen laughed again. "I think you're hanging around here too much yourself, Dr. Linden. I'll see you tomorrow." Jen raced off down the road.

As Jen let herself into the house, she glanced at her watch. Mom wouldn't be home for hours. She was working a double shift. I've got just enough time to study up on somewhere exciting to talk about this afternoon, Jen thought, reaching for one of the many access discs cluttering her desk.

The computer hummed and whirred as Jen switched it into sensory mode. She entered and exited site after site after site. Exotic music from foreign lands vibrated through the speakers, and the smell of foreign foods wafted into her nostrils through the olfactoports. She expected a hand to come out of the computer screen at any moment and offer her a plate of steaming cassoulet or curried goat cheese.

Preferring pizza, Jen wandered into the kitchen. She pulled a quick-frozen DehydroPak Pizza out of the microfreeze and popped it into the laserwave.

While she waited for the pizza to rehydrate and heat, she noticed the headlines displayed on the Newsview screen in the center of the breakfast table.

> **Secret Papers Leaked from**
> **Future-Tech Laboratory**
> **Surprise Scientists**

Jen pushed the scroll button on the tabletop and began to read the article.

> *Scientists are concerned that information leaked from the controversial Future-Tech Laboratory could fall into the wrong hands. The alleged information leak fuels speculation that Future-Tech is about to release software capable of uploading humans and translating their molecules for download into different environments. As a result of the reported leak, security has been tightened around the compound. In related news, many travel agents, fearing this new software could jeopardize the multimillion-dollar travel business, threaten a boycott of the new technology.*

"Wow, no wonder Dr. Linden was so uptight today. I knew something was going on. I wouldn't mind getting my hands on that software," Jen said aloud, but she couldn't help wondering, was Dr. Linden involved somehow in the leak?

Jen was about to pick up her snack tray and go back to her room, but on a whim, she quickly scrolled down to the classifieds to check on computer sales.

An advertisement in the computer section caught her eye.

> *Upgrade Your Vision!*
> *For sale*
> *VR headsets, good condition*
> *Unimaginable Images Virtual Reality Arcade*

Jen's heart raced. Wow, that would be the next best thing to molecular travel, she thought. Maybe I could meet one of the kids from the chat room in a virtual reality setting.

Wolfing down the pizza, Jen dialed the contact number, asked a few questions, checked the balance on her credit chip, and headed out the door.

Jen's mom was home when she returned.

"Where have you been?" Mom called. "I was starting to worry."

"Nowhere special," Jen said, trying to slip into her bedroom. "I just went to the Tech Library to collect some research material."

Jen shoved the bag containing the VR set under her bed and went to the kitchen. Mom didn't like VR machines. She was always saying that most of the VR games promoted excessive violence.

Fair enough, Jen thought, but there *are* other uses for virtual reality. She had no interest in games. She just wanted to travel to exotic places and meet new people. How could Mom argue with that? Jen mused. She's always telling me to make new friends. How can I help it if a friend I find lives somewhere on the other side of the world?

CHAPTER 3

Jen looked at her watch. It would soon be time to enter the chat room. She scrolled through different time zones until she reached Universal Standard Time. Not too long to wait, she thought. There's just enough time to check out my new purchase.

She carefully unwrapped the headset with its built-in wraparound visor and tiny speakers, spread out the set of instructions, and read them carefully.

The man at the Unimaginable Images Arcade had explained to Jen how the VR set worked. He had pointed out the delicate lenses in the visor, which would beam pictures from the computer into her eyes, and explained how the headset would track her movements so the view would change as she turned her head.

Jen's heart was racing. She wondered if she was doing the right thing after all.

She secured the last few connections, then looked through the small silver VR travel discs the man had thrown in for good measure – Kathmandu, Timbuktu, Under the Sea, Outer Space, Africa, Asia. Jen closed her eyes, picked a disc, and slipped it into the VR drive. She adjusted the visor and sat back.

A loud buzzing sounded in her ears and a bright light appeared before her eyes. Jen felt as if she were floating, then she began to move – *fast*. An unbelievable scene appeared beneath her. She was flying over the African veldt! The land parted and lagoons and waterways opened below. Animals raced beneath her and birds raced alongside her. Jen reached out and touched a bird's wing. Never in her wildest dreams could she have imagined this.

Just as quickly as it had started, it was all over. The scene dissolved and Jen felt herself landing. The lights went out and the sound died. What had seemed like an hour-long adventure had in fact taken only a few minutes.

"Unbelievable!" Jen cried. She glanced at her watch. It was getting late. She hoped that Amanda would still be waiting in the room.

Jen quickly connected, retrieved her IDENTIKIT picture and username, and entered the chat room.

> **Amanda Moveover:** *You're late. I was beginning to wonder if you were going to show.*
>
> **Sidney Sidewinder:** *You'll never guess what I just bought...*

When Jen told Amanda about her purchase, Amanda burst into an excited reply.

> **Amanda Moveover:** *You're not going to believe this. I've got an almost identical set. They were being sold by the army after being used to create VR scenes to train troops for all sorts of war situations.*
>
> **Sidney Sidewinder:** *What do you think would happen if we both linked up to the same site at the same time?*
>
> **Amanda Moveover:** *Let's try it. We'll meet at the African Adventure World Virtualpage on the Travel Seekers site.*

> **Sidney Sidewinder:** *I guess there's nothing to lose.*
>
> **Amanda Moveover:** *We'd better synchronize our watches. It's 18:20 hours Universal Standard Time now. Let's connect at 18:30 hours UST. If we don't meet up, send me an e-mail or meet in the chat room this time tomorrow.*

Amanda sent Jen her e-mail address and signed off.

"Sorry, Fireball. I can't take you with me," Jen told her kitten, which had sidled up beside her and begun meowing. "What's up with you, anyway? Do you hear something?" Jen strained her ears. All she could hear was her mom working in the kitchen.

"Stop making all that noise. It's only a VR headset. I'm not really going anywhere."

Jen looked at her watch. She would plug into the Simple Search Engine to make her way quickly to the African Adventure World Virtualpage. After hot-wiring the VR drive into the base of the computer screen, Jen put on the headset, and at exactly 18:30 UST, she pressed the "Send" button.

A strange sensation immediately came over her. Flashing lights spiraled and sparked in a misty tunnel before her. A series of strange monotonous sounds hummed through her earphones. She thought she could smell something burning. Her head began to spin and she suddenly felt as light as a feather as she moved rapidly through a darkened inner space.

There was a feeling of weightlessness as the lights dimmed and altered and the dim outline of the African veldt shimmered and sparked around her. Jen could see a figure fading in and out of view. It was someone her own age – a girl of about eleven, with thick, blonde curly hair and pale skin. "Amanda? Amanda?" she called, but she couldn't even hear her own voice. The faint figure hovered, calling soundlessly to her. Suddenly, Jen caught sight of another figure in what looked like a billowing robe. It seemed to be motioning to her. Then everything disappeared in a sudden blaze of static.

Jen felt a violent shock course through her body. She jerked upright and shook off the headset. Her computer screen showed nothing but static. No matter what she said or pressed, nothing appeared on the screen. What could have happened? Had the system crashed? She took a deep breath. Her heart raced. She pressed the reset button at the base of the screen and crossed her fingers. The computer flickered and hummed before settling into its screensaver mode.

Jen couldn't figure out what had caused the problem. Was the VR interface faulty? She lay on her bed watching the screensavers until she dropped off to sleep.

Late that night, Jen woke to Fireball's frantic cries. The kitten was sitting at the window and yowling at something outside. Jen hopped off the bed, rubbing sleep from her eyes. She was heading over to the window when the urgently blinking e-mail icon caught her eye.

Amanda! Jen rushed over to the computer screen. She tapped the envelope icon and watched it unfold.

Sidney–

Are you OK? I couldn't contact you after our encounter. There was some kind of disturbance on our street. The peacekeepers were out searching for something. Everyone was evacuated from their homes and taken to a bomb shelter. It was late by the time we were allowed to come back. What happened? I hope it was nothing to do with our connection. Maybe some kind of defragmentation occurred. The image I saw was a girl – twelvish, frizzy red hair. Was that you? You were obviously using an IDENTIKIT picture in the chat room. So was I. Did you see me? And did you see that weird shadowy thing? It seemed to be waving. What's up with that?

–Amanda

Peacekeepers? Bomb scares? Jen felt confused. She had figured that Amanda was just another kid like her. But where on earth did she live? What's more, she had seen the figure, too. Maybe it had something to do with the interrupted connection. Jen quickly e-mailed a reply.

> *Amanda–*
>
> *You saw me, the red-haired wonder.*
> *I guess we were both fooling each other.*
> *I have no idea what went wrong. Maybe it was an equipment or software failure, or some kind of atmospheric disturbance. We've had a bunch of thunderstorms lately. I don't know what that strange shadowy thing was. Maybe it was created by the interference, not the other way around. I could smell something burning when I connected. Do you think we should try again? I've got a friend at Future-Tech. I'll ask her advice. I'll be in touch same time tomorrow.*
>
> *–Sidney*

Jen was signing off when she heard something clatter against her window. Fireball's cries grew more desperate. Jen went to the window, looked out, and gasped. There in the backyard stood Dr. Linden, draped in an overcoat and wearing a hat, standing next to a weird little box topped by a small satellite dish.

Jen threw a jacket on and made her way quietly downstairs and out the back door. "Dr. Linden, what are you doing here? What's with the crazy getup?" Jen wasn't sure herself whether she meant the overcoat and hat or the satellite box.

"I'm sorry about what happened, Jen. I didn't realize the interference would be so profound."

"What are you talking about, Dr. Linden?"

The scientist motioned to the box. "This is a portable remote VR interface. I was scanning your VR transmission and tried to interject myself into your virtual reality journey so we could talk. The satellite dish picked up some secondary interference and the connection broke down. It disrupted your journey completely."

Jen remembered the shadowy figure she had seen during the VR experience.

She couldn't help feeling nervous. What was Dr. Linden up to?

As if reading her mind, Dr. Linden drew closer. "Don't worry, Jen," she said. "I just need your help. The rumor you heard about the new molecular transfer software program is true – at least some of it is. I designed the software myself, and I was working with Future-Tech to take the program through final trial stages. But someone in my lab section aided a hacker from another government to locate the software and get away with some top-secret information."

"Did they get away with everything?" Jen asked breathlessly.

"No," replied Dr. Linden. "But since then, all further development has been very carefully guarded. I spoke to my superiors and we came up with a scheme to hide the rest of the software development. Publicly, they blamed the security leak on me and demoted me to security to teach me a lesson. Actually, all the work on the software within the lab is a sham. I'm doing the real work in the security station."

Jen gasped and Dr. Linden let out a low laugh. "All the vehicle movement and trade-offs you've been seeing have been a red herring to suggest that I'm dissatisfied and disloyal. We're hoping to lull the real culprits into a false sense of security so they give themselves away."

"But what does this have to do with me?" Jen asked.

"We need to set up more trials, but for the reasons I've just stated, we can't do it at the lab. It would tip off the spy. I can't do it either. If someone catches wind of me doing anything except sitting in that station, it would blow the whole scheme right out of the water."

Dr. Linden placed her hand on Jen's shoulder. "That's where I thought you might come in. You're well beyond suspicion and your low body mass is ideal. Think of it, you could help us do one of the final trials and meet your new friend in the flesh!"

She handed Jen a disc. "If you insert this into your VR drive, we can transport you to Amanda. If that works, we can move to Phase Two – moving both of you to an entirely different location."

Jen couldn't believe her ears.

"I know it sounds tricky, Jen, but there is very little that can go wrong. We've already completed all the test trials. We just need a few final tests, then the world can know about it."

Jen felt dizzy. It was like a gigantic mixture of all the sci-fi and mystery novels she'd ever read. "Let's do it," she replied.

Dr. Linden nodded. "You'll need to memorize the code I'm going to give you, then start the trial immediately. The drive will give you instructions on everything from uploading yourself to downloading and returning home again. I want you to wear this bracelet. It has a Global Positioning Satellite chip so I can use this remote unit to track you at all times."

Dr. Linden gave Jen a hug. "Be careful, Jen. But know I'll be watching over you."

She picked up the satellite unit and disappeared into the night.

Jen rushed back into her bedroom and locked the door. She slipped the disk into the VR drive, which was still wired into the computer, and entered the code. In an instant a list of instructions played over the computer screen. Jen read them carefully and followed the commands. Finally, she disconnected the VR unit from the computer, put on the headset, entered Amanda's e-mail address into the drive, and pressed the "Send" button.

Immediately, Jen felt both hot and cold at the same time, and tiny shivers traveled through every inch of her body. A hazy fog obscured her vision. She felt as if she were flying, then floating, then slowly sinking. The fog thickened and, for a fleeting second, Jen felt as if she *were* the fog. She tried to reach out, but she couldn't feel anything.

Suddenly, the fog cleared and Jen's feet hit a solid surface. She looked around. She was in a small room containing nothing except a simple computer, an old desk, and a single bed. A plain blanket covered a sleeping shape. Jen took a step toward the bed then stopped, arrested by the scene outside the window. A dry, broken landscape spread out before her. The shattered remains of houses were scattered among mounds of twisted rubble and wrecked dusty streets. It reminded Jen of some of the war-torn villages she had seen on Viewscreen SatNet telecasts.

Amanda's reference to peacekeepers and bomb shelters was beginning to make sense. For a moment, Jen was tempted to wake the sleeping shape, but she had set the transfer timer for a mere five minutes, and already she could feel the hot and cold tingling in her limbs that signaled the return trip.

Meeting Amanda will have to wait, Jen decided as the room disappeared into a fog and she felt herself floating and flying once again. The return trip was as unsettling as the first. It was like being trapped inside a swirling thundercloud at the height of a storm.

Moments later, she was back in her room, lying on the bed with her headset on. She took it off and lay there looking into the darkness. How can I sleep? she thought. Tomorrow evening's never going to get here.

The next evening, Amanda signed on moments after Jen entered the room. Both of them still retained their IDENTIKIT aliases and usernames.

> **Sidney Sidewinder:** *Have I got something to tell you! Let's shift to a high-security private chat room.*
> **Amanda Moveover:** *Sure thing, but what's up?*

Jen sent Amanda an encrypted set of instructions for accessing a private room. Once there, they both engaged a security and encryption screen to mask their conversation. Then they switched off their IDENTIKIT aliases and posted their real images. Jen found herself looking at Amanda's dark smiling eyes framed by blonde ringlets of hair. Jen spoke into the computer. *Who are you?* scrolled onto the screen.

The smiling eyes sparkled. *Alexia, and you?*
Jen.
OK, Jen. Spill the beans. What's so exciting?

Jen quickly described her strange encounter with Dr. Linden and told Alexia about the molecular transfer software that allowed her to journey to Alexia's room.

Right, pull my other leg now, will you?

It's true. Listen, I'll describe your bedroom.

Jen watched Alexia's eyes get larger and larger by the minute.

Whoa, that's too much.

What's more, we can probably attempt a dual molecular transfer. Just think, you and I can beam to somewhere exciting.

I'd settle for peaceful.

Jen heard footsteps approaching her door. She spoke quickly: *I have to go, but I'll catch you same time tomorrow.*

Jen's mom entered the room just as she was signing off.

"You're not still on that thing, are you, Jen?" she said. "I ought to unplug it. I feel as if I never see you anymore. I know I work long hours, but I don't want you cooped up in your room every night. It can't be good for you. Maybe you could join a soccer team at school. I can't stand the thought of you alone here all the time."

45

Jen sighed and put her arm around her mom. "It's OK, Mom," she said, "I'm having fun and I am making friends – honest!"

Mom sighed and gave her a hug. "Oh well, just another week of these double shifts and it'll all be back to normal. You sleep tight." Mom shut off the light and slipped out the door.

Early the next morning, as Jen was getting ready for school, she heard a clatter at her window. When she looked out, Dr. Linden waved for her to come down.

"Great work," Dr. Linden said when Jen came outside. "I locked in on you with the tracking device last night. You made a successful molecular transfer to somewhere near Belgrade. I couldn't pinpoint exactly where. We're still having some problems with interference."

"So what's next?" Jen asked enthusiastically.

"Phase Two, I guess," Dr. Linden said. "Have you arranged to contact your friend tonight?"

"I sure have."

"You'll need to give her a set of matching coordinates. She won't have a disc, but that won't matter. As long as her coordinates are correct, you should both be downloaded to the same place. I suggest you transfer to a place you both know through the Travel Seekers site."

"Africa!" said Jen. "I can't wait. I'll arrange to meet at 18:20 UST."

"Let's do it then," Dr. Linden said.

Jen could hardly concentrate at school that day. As soon as she got home she sent an e-mail to Alexia: *Urgent. Meet in the private chat room 18:20 UST.*

Time dragged as Jen waited. She scrolled through the tabletop Newsview and picked at her dinner. Mom wouldn't be home for hours, and Fireball was in the other room, curled up asleep on a chair.

Jen looked at her watch: 18:15 UST. She went to her room, logged on, and entered the chat room. Alexia was waiting. She looked tired. Jen gave her the set of coordinates and briefed her on programming the VR set.

> **Jen:** *We'll connect at exactly 19:00 UST. Let's sync our program clocks. I can't wait to see you. Bring some stuff with you so I can see what you're like.*

Jen signed off and gathered some of her things to show her new friend. She grabbed her backpack and loaded it up with the complimentary Moonrise Cosmetic Kit her mom had been given when she traveled Eclipse Class on the Solar Shuttle to Orbit 3 Science Station, some gum, and a magnifying glass. She crammed a selection of other items into her pack, including an old handheld GamePak 5000 with an assortment of games.

She looked around the room. Was there anything else? She looked at the bed. I'd better set it up so if Mom comes home before I'm back, she'll think I'm asleep, Jen thought. She stuffed some blankets under the covers and arranged the pillows. Stepping back, she studied the bed. It would look better with the lights out, she decided.

Moments later, she placed the disc in the VR drive, put on the headset, and entered the coordinates. Holding her breath, she pushed "Send."

Within seconds, Jen could feel the flashes of hot and cold and the prickling shivers. A ghostly haze fogged her vision and the rhythmic droning sounded in her ears. Jen's heart pounded. She could feel herself zooming along at breakneck speed. She could just make out a dark speck moving quickly toward her.

Just as the dark figure began to take shape, Jen felt an eerie tremor. There was a loud crash and with a sharp jolt, she stopped moving. There was a brilliant flash of light and a sudden explosion. Everything went blank.

Jen opened her eyes and looked around. There was nothing but endless desert, a stand of straggly trees, and a crumpled figure lying beside her. She crawled to the figure and began shaking it. "Alexia, is that you?"

Alexia's eyelids began to flutter.

"Alexia. It's Jen. Can you hear me?"

Slowly, Alexia pulled herself into a sitting position, then reached out and touched Jen. "You're real," she gasped. "Is this what was supposed to happen?"

"I don't know," said Jen. "I don't think so."

The two girls looked around. Rolling dunes stretched away from them in every direction.

"Where are we?" Alexia asked.

"I'm not sure," Jen replied. "We targeted a nature reserve in Africa. My guess is that we got close. I'm just not sure how close."

Jen could feel the intense heat of the sun beating down on her back. Prickles of sweat began to form on her forehead.

"What should we do now?" Alexia asked.

"I guess the first thing is to get out of the sun."

The girls moved toward the cluster of trees – the only prospect of shelter in this hostile landscape. They crouched under one tree's sparse foliage. The scant shade speckled their bodies.

"I won't need this jacket," said Jen, pulling it over her head.

Alexia read the slogan on Jen's T-shirt: Global Achievement Camp. Prepared for Life.

"What's that?" she asked.

"Oh, it's a camp where kids get together to develop skills and overcome challenges. It's not really my kind of thing, but Mom makes me go.

She thinks I spend too much time on the computer. I'm not sure it's done much for me. It certainly didn't prepare me for this."

"What's the problem?" Alexia asked, looking surprised. "You got us here. Now all you've got to do is get us home."

"I set the transfer timer for one hour," Jen said. "After that, we should transfer back to our homes. I thought it would give us time to get to know each other and have some fun. I didn't expect we'd be stuck in the middle of a desert with nothing to do."

"One hour's not so long," Alexia said. "It'll fly by. I'll tell you what. I'll fill you in on my life story. If you're still awake when I've finished, you can tell me yours."

Alexia began to tell Jen about her life. She told her about her freedom-fighting parents, who were killed during a peaceful demonstration, about living alone with her only relative, an elderly aunt, and about how difficult it was trying to lead a normal life in a war-torn country.

Jen felt a little ashamed when Alexia had finished. Being a red-haired nerd and living alone with her mom didn't seem so bad after all. I'm lucky I even get to go to camp, Jen thought. An image of her mom came into her head and tears welled up in her eyes. She began to sort through her backpack so Alexia wouldn't see her face.

"Hey, I've got some stuff to show you," Jen said as she emptied her backpack.

"Sorry, I didn't have much time, so I only brought a few things," Alexia said.

The girls pulled out their things and spread them on the ground.

"I grabbed these from my camp kit," said Jen, handing Alexia a pocketknife, a small first-aid kit, and a foil survival blanket, which was carefully folded into a tiny square and wrapped in plastic.

They picked their way through the items, chatting excitedly. There was Jen's credit chip, a pack of gum, the magnifying glass, an apple, a comic book Alexia had rolled up and secured with rubber bands, and Jen's cosmetic set, which held a nail file, makeup, a pair of small scissors, tweezers, and a small vial of perfume.

"Well," Alexia laughed. "If we're stuck here forever, we could always eat the apple, read the comic, and file our nails."

Jen looked at her watch. "It's been an hour and a half!" she exclaimed. "We should have transferred back by now. Let's see. We connected at 19:00 UST exactly, so we should have transferred back at 20:00 hours."

"Are you sure you set the return time to UST?" Alexia asked.

"Yeah, at least I think I did. Maybe I didn't. I can't remember." Jen's head dropped and she again felt the stinging sensation of tears beginning to form.

Alexia reached out and touched her shoulder. "It's OK. Look, we're never going to last unless we can keep our wits about us. If the heat doesn't kill us, the boredom will."

"How long do you think we can survive if we don't get help?" Jen asked.

"I'm not sure," Alexia replied. "But we must do everything we can to make it as long as possible. We've got shade. What we need next is water."

"I've got an idea," Jen said. She crawled out from the shade and into an open area of sand, where she began to dig a small hole. "Give me the lid off the first-aid kit," she told Alexia. Jen placed the lid at the bottom of the hole and arranged several piles of leaves from the trees around it.

"What are you doing?" Alexia asked.

"I'm making a solar still," Jen replied. "It's one of the few things I remember from camp. Just keep your fingers crossed that it works."

Jen took the plastic wrapped around the survival blanket and carefully cut a piece from it with the nail scissors. She stretched it over the top of the hole. "Grab some of our stuff, Alexia," she said. "We can use it as weights to hold the plastic in place."

After they secured the edges of the plastic, Jen held her breath as she carefully placed a small rock in the center. The plastic dipped in the middle and stretched taut.

Alexia looked confused. "How is it supposed to work?"

"The sun's heat will evaporate moisture from the leaves in the still. The moisture condenses underneath the plastic and drops of water trickle down into the lid. If we leave it long enough it should provide us with at least a few sips of water."

"Pretty impressive!" Alexia said. "I just hope we don't have to stay here long enough to see if it really works."

The girls returned to the trees. "What else have we got that we can use?" Alexia asked, looking over the collection of items. "What about this old

GamePak? Maybe we could hot-wire the VR sets into this thing and send a message to Dr. Linden. It looks like it has a remote pickup on it."

"I don't know," Jen murmured. "It's pretty ancient."

"Hey, it's worth a try," said Alexia, flipping the top open.

There was a small flicker of light and a faint set of icons appeared on the screen.

"Well, there's hope after all," Alexia said. But before she could say anything else, the icons flickered and the screen went blank.

"So much for that idea," Jen said.

"The batteries must be dead," Alexia observed, flipping the lid down again. She paused. "What's this panel here? Hey, we can switch it to solar power! All this sun out here might actually be good for something." She set the small computer out in the sunlight. The digital readout got brighter and the icons reappeared.

"There we go," said Alexia. "See if you can send a message to Dr. Linden. I'm going to get some firewood."

"Firewood? It's too hot as it is!"

"It'll be cold when the sun goes down," Alexia said as she began gathering dead branches from under the trees.

Nervously, Jen hot-wired the VR sets into the GamePak and engaged the disc drive. She slowly typed "jlinden@future-tech.lab" in the address area. The Future-Tech contact details appeared on the screen and Jen typed in her message.

> *Attention, Dr. Linden–*
>
> *We suffered some kind of error in our coordinate placement and the transfer timer seems to have malfunctioned. We're stuck in the desert. We will not last long without food and water. Need details for urgent transfer back to our original locations.*

"Well, that's that," Jen said, pushing "Send." "There's nothing to do now but wait."

"I guess there is no point in sitting and doing nothing," Alexia said, putting down an armful of wood. "We might as well build a fire and get ready for nightfall."

Both girls looked up at the sky. The sun was getting lower.

"Maybe we should travel at night while it's cooler and try to find help," Jen said.

Alexia disagreed. "I don't think we should move from here. I think it's safer if we stay in the spot where the computer downloaded us. If we move, who knows if they'll ever be able to find us?"

They began to build a small pile of dead leaves and kindling a few feet from the tree. Jen stopped suddenly. "We don't have any matches," she said. "How are we going to light this?"

Alexia examined the items under the tree. "We can use that magnifying glass and the perfume. Here, shred some pieces of paper from this comic book."

Jen began tearing tiny pieces from the comic. When she was done, Alexia stuffed the paper loosely into the pile of leaves and twigs. Then she dowsed it liberally with the perfume. "Keep your fingers crossed," she said as she angled the magnifying glass to focus the sun's rays on the pile. A few moments later, the paper flared, and Alexia carefully began to feed twigs into the tiny flames.

"Way to go!" Jen said, helping her to nurse the fire along.

As the night grew colder, the girls fed the fire and huddled together, wrapping the survival blanket around them.

"Do you think we'll really make it back home?" Alexia asked.

"Sure," said Jen as her stomach rumbled with hunger. The girls shared the apple and the water collected in the still and finally dozed as the night drew on.

When they awoke, the sun was high in the sky. Jen reached halfheartedly for the GamePak and set it out in the sunlight.

It didn't take long for the desert sun to bring the small computer up to full power. The girls couldn't believe it when the e-mail icon began flashing urgently. Jen opened the icon.

I've got you two! There must have been some disruption at one of your initial transfer points. It created a variable in the coordinates and temporarily knocked out the transfer timer and Global Positioning chip. Once I received your message I was able to triangulate on your position. You are located on the edge of the Gobi desert. Follow these precise instructions and we should be able to download you both back to your original locations. Punch the following encrypted code and respective coordinates into your VR sets. Back it up by using your individual e-mail addresses. Then press the "Send" button.
Good luck!

–Dr. Linden

The girls followed Dr. Linden's instructions and entered the coordinates. When they were finished, Alexia looked at Jen. "Let's get rolling. It was great to meet you, but I hope it's not like this next time!"

"You know it," Jen replied. "Let's swap messages when we get home so we know we're both OK."

They secured their headsets. "Cross your fingers," Jen yelled as they both pushed "Send."

CHAPTER 7

Jen found herself lying on her bed. Her eyes wandered around her room. Everything was in order, just as she had left it. Fireball was meowing loudly at the foot of the bed, and Jen could hear her mother in the hallway. I'm home, Jen thought, taking off the headset. Boy, I don't want to do that again soon.

Her mother's voice came through the door. "Jen, are you getting up? Breakfast is almost ready."

"Coming, Mom," Jen said. She hid the VR set under the bed and went down for breakfast. It wasn't until after breakfast, when she was gathering her things for school, that she thought of Alexia.

Alexia lay stunned. Every so often another layer of plaster would fall from above, showering her with powdery dust. She moved some rubble from around her. Everything was deathly quiet. Her eyes slowly grew accustomed to the half-light. Well, this explains the disruption, she thought to herself. Only a bomb could do this much damage.

She called out, but there was no reply. She was trapped within the crumbled concrete and twisted metal that had once been her room. She carefully lifted some of the debris from around her and cleared a small space, trying to locate her computer system. Perhaps if she could get it working, she could call for help. Finally, she located it. It seemed to be intact, although the console was badly dented. She tried to switch it on. The screen remained dark. "Useless," Alexia murmured. "It won't work without power."

Then she remembered the EvacPak, an emergency survival pack that her aunt kept stored in Alexia's closet. Careful not to disturb any of the precariously balanced debris, she made her way to the far side of the room. She felt around in the closet until she located the EvacPak. To her relief, it contained a BattPak emergency power generator.

Alexia connected the BattPak to the computer and turned it on. The screen flickered to life. She prepared an emergency e-mail for Jen and pressed "Send."

Jen was about to leave her room for school when the e-mail icon began to flash. Alexia! she thought. She touched the icon and read the message.

> *Jen, are you back? Anyone? Need help. Urgent. There's been a bombing.*

Jen quickly connected to the Travel Seekers site and selected the nearest location she could find. She locked in the coordinates and spoke a reply to Alexia's e-mail.

> *Prepare to reconnect. Set your VR set to the encrypted coordinates. Connect in exactly five minutes at 07:30 UST.*

Alexia sat perfectly still, afraid that any sudden movement would send the remains of her room crashing down on top of her. Her heart raced when she saw the e-mail icon flashing. She downloaded the coordinates, secured the VR headset, and counted the seconds. At exactly 07:30 UST, she pushed "Send."

Jen and Alexia could see each other spinning through the vortex of light and fog. In a blinding whirl, they passed one another, each catching a glimpse of the other's stricken face. Jen felt a sudden jerk. She could feel her body hovering, twisting, then slowly reversing.

She turned her head to see where she was going. Alexia swirled past again and Jen put out both her hands and grabbed at her friend's shirt as she passed. The two girls clung together as they whirled and spun and tumbled to a stop.

Jen rubbed at her eyes and looked at Alexia. Their faces were bathed in a gaudy rainbow of flashing light. "That sure didn't feel like last time,"

Jen said. She paused. "You look terrible, Alexia. Are you all right?"

"I think so," Alexia replied. "Where are we?"

The girls stared at each other and then looked up. A large neon sign flickered on and off above them.

"This doesn't look like my coordinates," said Jen. "We should have ended up in Yosemite."

Alexia tried to read the flashing sign. "What does that say? It's some kind of hieroglyphics."

Bewildered, Jen looked around at the bleak urban landscape. "Well, what are we going to do now?"

Before Alexia could give Jen an answer, two figures appeared further down the street. Jen grabbed Alexia's arm and they ducked into a small alley. They pressed up against a wall, too afraid to move. The figures came nearer. Their voices were a deep murmur and the language was totally unfamiliar.

The figures stopped and looked down the alley. Neither girl breathed. At last, the figures moved on.

"Come on," said Alexia. "Let's follow them."

"Why?" Jen whispered.

"Maybe we can figure out where we are."

The girls shadowed the two moving shapes out into the street. All the storefronts were dark except for flashing signs with strange lettering. When Jen tried to look in a window, she could see only her own reflection. The two dark forms hurried along ahead of them. There were no other signs of life.

"Where is everyone?" Alexia asked.

"Beats me," said Jen. "This place is weird."

Suddenly a piercing siren sounded behind them. The two figures they were following ducked into a doorway and disappeared. Jen and Alexia looked desperately in every direction. There was nowhere to hide.

An armored vehicle came gliding down the road, its bright spotlight swinging from doorway to doorway, searching like a giant eye. It caught the girls in its beam and the wailing siren stopped abruptly. The two girls pressed together, not knowing what might happen next.

Panels on either side of the vehicle began to rise like giant wings. Before the girls knew what was happening, a mesh net sprung from the vehicle's side. When it was directly over their heads, it stopped in midair, unfurled into a cylindrical shape, and settled down around them, surrounding them in its embrace. A heavyset man stepped out of the vehicle and walked toward them. He seemed to be a police officer, but his face was hidden behind a dark, gauzelike metal visor that

descended from his helmet. The man said something unintelligible in a gruff, menacing voice.

"We can't understand you," said Jen.

The man moved slowly closer. With a quiet humming noise, the mesh net parted and he stepped through.

"We didn't mean to cause any trouble," Alexia said.

The man reached into his pocket and pulled out a small black box, which he pointed toward the girls. "Don't hurt us! We didn't do anything!" Jen cried, grabbing Alexia's arm.

As she spoke, the box began to follow her words with words in the strange language, pausing when she paused. The man listened, then looked at the digital readout on the black box. He pressed a few buttons and spoke to the girls again. This time, the box translated his words into English. "Who are you? What are you doing out roaming the streets at night? Are you not aware of the penalties for breaking curfew?"

"What do you mean 'curfew'? Where are we?" Jen asked.

The man spoke again. "I am an Enforcer. You are in Oceanic Sphere 4. You will need to empty your pockets now."

The girls did as they were told.

The Enforcer looked over the items. "What is this? An ancient GamePak! I have seen these things only on history discs. Where did you get one of these?"

Jen and Alexia tried to tell him their story but the Enforcer cut them off. "Many strange stories, many strange ideas. I hear them all the time. The conservationists are always trying to distract us while they attempt to prevent the radiothermoactive plants from expelling waste into the ocean."

Jen and Alexia looked at each other bewildered.

"The ocean! You do understand me? Look!" The Enforcer pointed up. Far above them was a dome, and beyond the dome was water. They could just make out the dark shapes of seaweed and fish.

"You are in Oceanic Sphere 4. You will now come with me," the Enforcer said. He pointed a small remote control device at his vehicle and the mesh net surrounding the girls collapsed, folding into a small packet that the Enforcer picked up and reinserted into an opening in the vehicle's side.

"Get in," he said, gesturing at the vehicle.

Jen looked around. She thought of making a run for it, but even if she escaped the Enforcer, there was nowhere to go. The girls were trapped far beneath the surface of the ocean. They had run out of options.

Jen and Alexia sat on a bench in the rear of the vehicle, secured by padded safety harnesses that the Enforcer clicked into place over their arms and legs. The Enforcer entered a code on the panel in front of him and the vehicle began to glide effortlessly along the road. Its route was shown as a flashing neon dot on a glowing map displayed over the Enforcer's head.

"What are we going to do?" Alexia whispered.

Jen shrugged. "I'm not sure what to do. I don't know where we are. I don't even know *when* we are."

Eventually, the vehicle glided to a halt. The doors raised and the girls were led out. They found themselves in a large underground room, with one wall entirely covered by computer and video screens. An Enforcer sat at a central console in front of the wall, his hooded face turned toward the screens in front of him.

Another uniformed Enforcer walked up. "What have we got here?" he asked, the black box translating his words.

"I'm not sure," the first Enforcer replied. "They seem to be something out of the Dark Ages."

The second man took out a small contraption that looked like a Geiger counter and held it in front of the two girls. It clicked and whirred as its screen flashed a series of numbers. "They look pretty clean to me," he said. "No sign of radiothermoactive contamination. But why were they wandering around after curfew? Don't they know the dangers of being outside while radiothermoactive wastes are being expelled into the ocean?"

The Enforcers sat the girls on a bench and placed the voice translator in front of them. Jen and Alexia tried once more to explain their situation. The men remained impassive. Finally, the first Enforcer led the girls into a small room containing two bare concrete slabs and a small metal sink. As he passed out of the room, he pressed something in the wall and another mesh barrier covered the doorway.

Jen and Alexia sat on the slabs, too frightened to move.

After what seemed like ages they heard the hum of the mesh net collapsing.

Neither girl recognized the voices of the two men who now entered the room speaking urgently to each other. Jen strained to understand what they were saying, but without the voice translator she could only guess.

The taller man handed Jen the items that had been confiscated from them. The girls were relieved to have the GamePak and VR sets, but they didn't know what they were going to do with them. Then they were led to another vehicle, which slowly made its way out of the underground building and into the open. The underwater city was now lit by a radiating globe set at the apex of the dome, and for the first time, the girls were able to take a good look around. Strange vehicles glided noiselessly along the roads. People dressed exactly alike moved around in an orderly fashion.

The vehicle stopped outside a large monochrome building. The doors raised and the girls were ushered out.

"Where do you suppose they're taking us?" Alexia asked.

The building's main door slid open. Inside, the air was alive with technology. The outer walls were lined with rows of large computers. Dividers in the middle of the room created a huge maze, a combination of many hexagonal boxes, each enclosed by the familiar mesh barriers. Within each segment, people sat or lay down wearing what looked like small VR headsets. The noise was deafening as the people laughed, yelled, or called out to no one in particular.

Jen and Alexia were fascinated and frightened. "It's like a huge VR arcade," Jen whispered.

She felt a heavy hand on her shoulder. The taller Enforcer spoke into the translator he held in his hand. "This is Government Building 305, Reeducation and Replacement. These people are being reeducated. You will be replaced. Please follow me."

The Enforcers led them toward a huge computer screen on which satellite images flickered, held for a few seconds, then were replaced by other images. Coastlines and countrysides, cities and seascapes scrolled endlessly. Jen's heart lurched when several images of her own city flicked on the screen. She could see some familiar landmarks, but before she was able to place them, the images had changed to another city.

"That was home," she said to Alexia. "But everything seemed different."

Before she had a chance to say more, Alexia's eyes lit up and she let out a loud cry. Jen looked at the screen, which was zeroing in on a series of locations around one city.

Alexia pointed excitedly. "That's my home city, but without any damage. They rebuilt it, Jen, and it looks positively peaceful."

The shorter Enforcer laughed, adjusted the voice translator, and motioned at the screen. "Surface dwellers. They are all conservationists. We will not tolerate their kind here."

The taller Enforcer cut in. "You said you came here via ancient technology. We will now send you back using our modern technology. You are displaced. We cannot tolerate you here. Your kind puts an unnecessary strain on our sphere."

Jen and Alexia looked at the Enforcers, then at each other. "It's all very well telling us we're not wanted, but what can we do?" Jen asked.

A large man dressed in a heavy looking leaded garment approached them.

"That must be to prevent radiation sickness from prolonged exposure to all these machines," Alexia whispered to Jen.

"Who is first?" the man asked gruffly.

The girls stared.

"Well, come on," the man continued. "I do not have all day. Where and when do you have to go?"

"We can't hang around here all day," snapped the taller Enforcer, taking Jen by the shoulders and leading her toward a chair connected by a network of corrugated wiring to an enormous computer.

"Very well, then," said the man in the leaded garment, forcing Jen into the chair and securing some straps around her legs and arms. "Present your bar code chip for identification scanning."

Jen shrugged. "Bar code?"

"Your personal bar code ID chip. The one inserted in your forearm," he said impatiently. "Replacement is available only for the displaced. All others are to be reeducated. I cannot transfer anyone without recording a personal ID code. I might be reeducated myself."

The tall Enforcer moved closer. "You will send them by patching through their VR headsets."

"Those ancient things?" the man said in utter disbelief.

"You will do it," said the Enforcer.

Looking frightened, the man complied. He wired Jen's VR headset into some ports on the chair. "I am going to impose a temporal homing signal over your original program," he explained. "You wish to go home, don't you?"

Jen looked at Alexia, who nodded and smiled. "But what if no one finds you?" Jen asked her.

"You can let them know where I am, Jen. I just want to go home."

Jen turned back to the man. "Yes," she said. "We want to go home."

The man pushed a series of buttons on the chair and the computer started humming and whirring.

Jen looked over at Alexia. "See you in the real world." The tingling coursed through her body and the room disappeared.

CHAPTER 10

"Where have you been?" It was Mom's voice. "I swear you weren't there a minute ago. And what is that on your head?"

Jen sat up on her bed, wrestling off the headset. Her mother anxiously rushed over and gave her a hug. "I came in to get you for school, but you weren't here. I knew you hadn't left the house. If I didn't know better, I'd say you'd disappeared. I've been looking everywhere!"

"Mom," Jen said. "I'm OK, honest. And I'll explain everything, but right now I need to find out if Alexia's all right."

"Who's Alexia?"

"Mom, I will explain. I promise I will. I just need to…" Jen's voice trailed off. From the Viewscreen in the other room she could hear a newscaster's voice.

It was a catastrophe waiting to happen. Just days into the latest cease-fire, the government militia began their most vicious attack yet. Bombing continued throughout the night, and now little remains of this small town in Eastern Europe and its innocent civilians. Peacekeepers were able to reenter the region earlier today, but rescuers have little hope of finding survivors.

"That has to be where Alexia lives," Jen said, grabbing her mom's arm. "We've got to help them find her."

"But you don't know anyone named Alexia," Mom said.

"Please, Mom, you've got to listen. Alexia's my e-mail friend. Well, she's really… I mean… It doesn't matter… We've just got to find out if she's all right."

Mom looked at her. "I think you've been spending far too much time on that computer, but I'll bite. What do you want me to do?"

"Take me to Dr. Linden, Mom. She can help us, and I'm sure she can explain everything."

Alexia opened her eyes and looked around. Nothing had changed. She was no better off than when she had returned from the desert. She thought of trying to hook up with Jen again, but shook her head. I'm not going to connect again, she thought. Who knows where I'd end up? It might be somewhere even worse, though that's hard to imagine! She found a blanket among the rubble and huddled beneath it.

Jen and her mom drove up to the entrance of Future-Tech Laboratory. To Jen's amazement, at least a dozen police cars surrounded the gates. There were three or four other black cars parked by the gate, too. People in dark suits and sunglasses leaned against them.

Jen made her way over to the security station. Dr. Linden was there, her attention glued to the monitor

in front of her. Information was scrolling down the screen. She seemed to be searching for something frantically.

"Dr. Linden!" Jen shouted as she burst into the security station.

Dr. Linden looked up. An expression of intense relief passed over her face. "Oh, thank goodness," she said. "What happened to you, Jen? Where did you go? When you uploaded again, I lost you completely. Whatever disrupted the transfer must have been very violent. I've never seen readings quite like that."

Jen quickly explained what had happened. Dr. Linden's jaw dropped open when Jen told her about their journey to the undersea city.

"Time displacement!" Dr. Linden exclaimed. "Think of the possibilities!"

"Dr. Linden, we need to find Alexia. The disruption was caused by a bombing. She's trapped and she needs our help."

"Of course, Jen." Dr. Linden turned back to the screen and traced the coordinates for Alexia's position. The computer was unable to locate her.

"The grid there must be badly damaged," said Dr. Linden. "What's her e-mail address?"

Jen gave it to her, then watched as Dr. Linden frantically sent off a message to Alexia.

Alexia couldn't believe it when she saw a pale e-mail icon flicker on her screen. She reached out slowly and touched it, afraid that any sudden movement might make it disappear. The icon unfolded and the words stood out on the screen.

Reply please. Remote tracer attached.
Will track signal for exact location.

Alexia pushed "Send Reply" just as the last remaining beam propping up the roof collapsed with a bang. There was a sudden weight on her back and everything went black.

As soon as the return e-mail came through, Dr. Linden notified the search-and-rescue authorities in Alexia's city. Then the three of them waited anxiously. While they waited, Dr. Linden explained that the person who had been leaking information from the lab had just been caught. "He tried to pass the fake copy of the program off to an undercover agent. They caught him red-handed."

Taking turns, Jen and Dr. Linden then tried to explain to Jen's mom everything that had happened.

As the minutes slowly passed, Jen felt more and more horrible. She felt as if she had abandoned Alexia to her fate. After thirty minutes, there was still no word. Jen wondered if she would ever see Alexia again.

An hour passed... and still nothing. Finally, Mom spoke, "I'm really sorry, Jen, but we'd better go home."

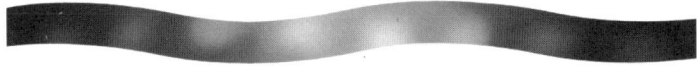

As soon as they arrived home, Jen ordered the Viewscreen to come on. An announcer's urgent voice immediately cut through the air.

> *One day after the devastating bombing of an East European city, a young girl has been recovered from the ruins of a bombed-out apartment building. The child, now being referred to as the Internet Angel, was discovered after an e-mail friend alerted authorities to her whereabouts.*

Jen leaped up in joy. Viewscreen footage showed Alexia being lifted out of the rubble by paramedics and carried on a stretcher to a waiting Airsled for evacuation.

> *The girl, said to be the only family survivor, is in fair condition and will be cared for by authorities until a suitable placement is found. In related news, the government has today confirmed that five more countries have agreed to accept refugees until the newly signed peace settlement is in place...*

Jen whooped with excitement as the phone rang. It was Dr. Linden.

"Jen, did you hear?"

"I heard, Dr. Linden. I heard! She's OK. Alexia's OK!"

"Not only that, Jen," said Dr. Linden, "but Future-Tech has taken a personal interest in Alexia's plight. They are willing to pay to fly her over and arrange for her care. They're also willing to sponsor her for placement. We've already had several people step forward to adopt her."

Jen didn't know what to say.

Dr. Linden continued. "I think you, Alexia, and Future-Tech will have a bit of work to do together in the future, Jen. Just think of it – time travel! What do you say?"

"You bet!" Jen replied enthusiastically.

When Jen hung up, she bent down and picked up her kitten. "Come on, Fireball, let's get my credit chip. I'm going down to Unimaginable Images to pick up a dual-port VR set. Once Alexia gets here, we've got places to go!"

GLOSSARY

DehydroPak – food packaging in which all moisture is drawn out of a food item and stored in the packaging. Moisture is released back into the food when heated. This allows food to be stored indefinitely.

EvacPak – an emergency supply package containing a BattPak power source, dehydrated food, water, and blankets

GamePak – a flip-top handheld computer used for games and remote communication

Global Positioning Satellite – a method of location involving satellite tracking

IDENTIKIT – a cyberspace resource for setting up an alternative identity

laserwave – similar to a microwave, but using lasers to cook food

microfreeze – a freezer using reverse microwave technology to freeze food

Newsview – a cyberspace "newspaper" provided free to computer users

olfactoports – ports on computers allowing users to experience cyberspace smells

Perspex – "smart" plastic that allows for handprint scanning, among other uses

retinal scan – a method of identification that maps the network of blood vessels at the back of a person's eyes. No two people share the same pattern of retinal blood vessels.

SatNet – a satellite news network

Universal Standard Time (UST) – similar to Greenwich Mean Time, but providing for time standardization between Earth, the moon, and space station time zones

Viewscreen – similar to a television screen, but wall-mounted and voice-activated

FROM THE AUTHOR

I love using e-mail and the Internet to learn about the world and to make new friends. One day I connected to a web site for writers and entered a chat room. It was a great experience that made me want to write about an adventurous Internet friendship.

Of course, I had to call in some experts on the subject, and these twelve-year-olds were full of ideas and suggestions.

I'd like to thank these experts, my cyber-friends Oceane, Michael, Jonathon, Karl, Tuki, Bobby, and Francis, as well as Steve Outram, the computer technician at Te Puke Intermediate School, for their assistance in writing this story.

Angie Belcher

FROM THE ILLUSTRATOR

When I was at school, I used to choose books from the library that had cool illustrations. I kept checking out those same books over and over. I would spend a lot of time looking at the illustrations and examining them closely. I didn't realize it at the time, but the illustrations were encouraging me to read the story to see how the characters interacted and what was going to happen next.

I like to think that my illustrations are encouraging others to get into reading, just as the illustrations in the books that I used to read encouraged me.

Alan Cochrane

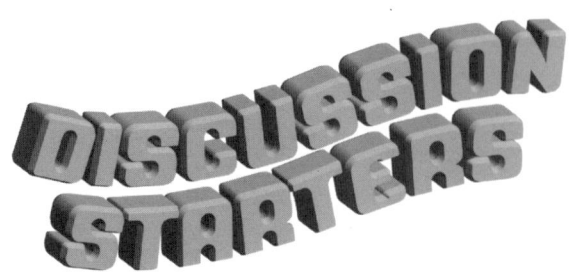

DISCUSSION STARTERS

1. If you had a virtual reality device and you could go anywhere you desired, where would you go? What would you like to see and do?

2. Chatting on the Internet can lead to danger. What are some things that a person in today's society can do to ensure safety from strangers? Discuss how the ideal IDENTIKIT would work and how it could be used in today's version of cyberspace.

3. Dr. Linden suggests that Jen and Alexia might do some more work with Future-Tech. If you were Jen's mother, how would you react to this suggestion?